The author holds a Master's degree in chemistry with a Postgraduate Diploma in Marketing Management and has abundant work experience spanning 33 years in different countries, with a majority in the Middle East. Specialises in sales with a job profile involving selling specialty chemicals techno-commercially in the MEA region. A reputed public speaker and has conducted product presentations on marketing and technical topics in various global forums. He is a recent enthusiast on the topic of Sustainability. He likes travelling around the globe and is a keen observer of cross-cultural business perspectives.

Sachin Arte

SALESMAN BY CHANCE

AUSTIN MACAULEY PUBLISHERS™

LONDON • CAMBRIDGE • NEW YORK • SHARJAH

ISBN – 9789948770206 – (Paperback)
ISBN – 9789948770213 – (E-Book)

Application Number: MC-10-01-8798122
Age Classification: E

Printer Name: iPrint Global Ltd
Printer Address: Witchford, England

First Published 2024
AUSTIN MACAULEY PUBLISHERS FZE
Sharjah Publishing City
P.O Box [519201]
Sharjah, UAE
www.austinmacauley.ae
+971 655 95 202

Table of Contents

Prologue

This book is dedicated to all the companies and organizations that had a great influence in shaping the way I am today and narrates my biographical journey in the profession of sales.

To my departed parents and my wife Manisha, who has been a rock-solid support during the "head and tail winds" of various challenges in life, and our son Aditya, who was quite an important support in the endeavor.

I would also like to mention a few names who helped me in my journey, and without naming them in the book would have been an incomplete endeavor.

Narendra Kulkarni, my childhood friend who always motivated me to narrate the journey of my experience compiled in a short book covering my business travels and the learnings around the globe.

My friend, philosopher, and guide OA, who has long retired from the company where I am currently working, contributed profoundly to my understanding of the philosophy of buying and selling and the psychology of selling during our various encounters with challenging situations during travel around the world for business.

Dr. KB, one of the best man managers I was fortunate to work with, who is unfortunately no longer a colleague but more of a family friend and had imparted the best practices of employee empowerment and taking fast decisions in the field.

Another family friend, Siddharth Shah, who remains a person I can depend for support and advice in the topsy-turvy world of uncertainty in the good and bad times. Last but not least, MS, a friend and one of the finest sales professionals and a great human being I have met in my life.

However, certain names of individuals and organizations are changed to protect their identity and privacy. It would be an injustice of not mentioning all the names of the companies, colleagues, and clients I worked with, but that may have turned out to be impractical judging by the long, unending list.

The book mainly covers the major professional life I was fortunate to experience in the Middle East – United Arab Emirates and in Sultanate of Oman during my domicile and traveling around the whole of the Middle East and parts of the world.

Hence, I would like to make a statement in Arabic, "Ana Khaleej ana Hada Hayati," which translates to **My Gulf (Middle East) my life.**

Perhaps this vast experience can help young ambitious people out there in the field of sales to understand the intricacies of sales management, along with my takeaways, to emerge victorious in the ever-changing scenario of disruptions in the field, and to those who aspire to dream big!!!

Also wish to thank the publishers, Austin Macauley UAE, for making this dream a reality.

Foreword

27 years of selling experience condensed into 92 pages: what a "herculean task," to use the words of Sachin Arte, to enlighten the reader with so many memories and so much knowledge and conclusions in just a centimeter-thick stack of paper – or a millisecond of data transfer if you read electronically. Despite the unavoidable compression of that wealth, it expands on all key aspects of the sales process and its development over the advance of a career. It is, hence, of great practical value for any freshman in the field of sales and a source of joyful inspiration to look back on own endeavors for the seasoned sales manager. Or both for those of us who are at the center piece of their professional journey.

I had the pleasure to work with Sachin Arte throughout almost five years, during which we were both stationed at company's regional HQ in Dubai. During a two years' part of that period, we had to go through the challenge of the Covid-19 pandemic. Countermeasures to minimize the spread of the virus kept many salespeople away from their customers and prospects. That situation caused significant distress among many members of the crew. Not so for Arte. He embraced the opportunities arising from the crisis, outperformed his competition by creating the best possible remote experience for his leads, and was the first to be back in person with customers when it was permitted again. Having read this book, you will understand why he dealt so successfully with the imposed change of the customer interface. It is the positivity and dedication that characterized his entire approach to the task of selling – and life as such. Change is imminent to business life and even more so in sales jobs, as internal and external changes seem to multiply each other in their effects on business activities. Arte demonstrates how to deal with such change in a variety of circumstances, so the readers will be able to draw conclusions for most of their own critical situations. Regardless of how different Arte's experiences and his responses to issues may have been, there is one constant thought that he always adhered to: deep respect for the nature of humans. Sachin's love for people is at the heart of his approach. And, yes, at times that love was betrayed. However, Sachin held on to his very own idea of how to conduct his duties with positivism and perseverance. And it paid out in most cases, and in any case for his overall progress.

Attitude alone is not enough to be a successful salesperson in a business-to-business environment. Knowing your products and knowing your customer's application of them even better is the foundation of the sales task. Arte details this to a great extent, and it becomes obvious that his way of selling is a combination of science and art, of facts and faces, of diligence and vision. It may be a bit intimidating for the young reader to imagine the long path to follow before becoming a master of sales to that comprehensive extent. But Sachin Arte has the talent to draw the picture of that path in a way that can encourage and inspire a young sales apprentice without hiding the possibility of failure and frustration on that journey. If there was one learning from his experiences, it would be the conclusion that there is always a bigger learning from a failure. Hence, Arte's message to you stands out: Progress is certain if just we accepted obstacles as an opportunity to rise higher while stepping on them.

Dr. Hendrik Schoenfelder

Introduction to
My Formative Years

I was born as the single child in a lower middle-class family to working parents growing up in a megapolis called Mumbai.

My early childhood days were quite exciting because, as an only child, I was exceptionally pampered. My mother was a working woman in a municipal corporation school. She started working there as a primary school teacher, eventually retiring as headmistress of the school. My father was a senior ticket collector in the Indian Railways, and hence had a traveling job for most of his life.

I was raised by my mother, who was a very strong personality by nature, and it won't be an exaggeration to say that I was raised in a matriarchal household.

My childhood days were quite eventful, with schooling from a primary convent school followed by an English-medium secondary school.

In hindsight, I thank my parents for enrolling me in an English-medium school, judging the competition that was emerging in a hugely populous country such as India. With scarcity looming large for almost many essentials and with life emerging as an epic monumental struggle in those times, the only emancipation was possessing a reasonable education and skill level to secure a job and lead a normal life.

We stayed in a municipal tenement offered as part of my mother's employment at the school. I have vivid childhood memories of growing up with a lot of friends from our colony and neighborhood; a few of them remain my buddies till date and we remain in contact courtesy of the digital revolution and the social media phenomenon.

As I started to grow up, things became more challenging, as being a normal, average student, I was at times overwhelmed by the ocean of competition in school and college. To this day, I remember a comment from a coaching class teacher while preparing for higher secondary school certification examinations.

During his periodic frustration with me and another fellow student, he metaphorically compared us to the coffee grounds which people discard after brewing coffee, stating that my place in society and my future aspirations are just as pointless as those coffee grounds. He told me the students that contribute toward the welfare of society pass through the filters of the coffee machine to create a wonderful cup of coffee, while "trash" such as myself should be resigned to being discarded. This was quite a demotivating comment for a young boy on the threshold of new beginnings.

Never did I realize that the insults and insinuations would probably help me in the tough profession of sales many decades later, and hence, I would now thank my teacher for pushing me hard with the taunts and innuendos for enabling me to succeed in the modern rat race.

Let me be clear; I hold no malice toward my teacher, as it helped me to introspect and improve. It helped me shape my life. Hence, looking back in retrospect, the teacher wanted me to succeed and face the upheavals of life by excelling in academics.

As a pampered child, I took early life very easy, but things started to change after matriculation and stepping into the daunting challenge called college life. Regularly encountering failures and setbacks, I never gave up on my goal of finding a good job after college and decided to enroll in the science stream. Science was in demand back in the day, and there were plentiful employment opportunities.

Biology, Zoology, and Chemistry remained my favorite subjects in junior college, so I decided to pursue these subjects in higher college. However, mathematics remained quite a challenge for me.

I was also selected as the best student at my college in an academic year, which gave me the push, the motivation, and the confidence into transitioning from a shy introvert to later succeeding in the future decades in a highly extrovert field of sales.

I found that job opportunities would become easier to find with a bachelor's degree in Chemistry, so I chose it for my graduation and emerged successfully, graduating with flying colors. This success and adulation in the college gave me the momentum to work consistently toward all future goals.

After graduation, life tossed two options: a) sourcing a job or b) further studies by securing a post-graduation in chemistry.

I started my first job as a medical representative. I didn't anticipate how tough initially this job would be, primarily due to long hours of travel and meeting doctors in hospitals at odd times.

I discussed with my parents about the challenges of a prospective career as a Medical Representative, and they gave me the reassurance that I was on the right path in life if I put in the extra hours and efforts. However, they stressed the need for further education.

Even though both my parents had retired, they did not let the pinch of the expenses deter me from studying further and trying my post-graduation in chemistry. I enrolled back in college and was quite successful in securing a post graduate degree in chemistry.

The master's in science offered the courage to start my life with a steady job. The second job I received in my life was as a part-time lecturer/professor of chemistry at a junior college. It was at Mumbai's renowned college, albeit for a short term, as a replacement for a professor who was on maternity leave.

As the fundamentals of chemistry were quite strong and fresh, I was quite popular with the students and started cherishing the teaching profession as my career path, as it was in my genes, naturally passed on courtesy of my mother's profession as a teacher.

The pay was quite good for an aspiring youth, but the job remained short lived as the original lecturer, whom I replaced temporarily was back to resume her duty.

So, I was job hunting once again and applied for a position of R&D Chemist with one of the leading paint manufacturers in India through an advertisement in the newspaper.

I got selected and started my new phase as an R&D chemist. In hindsight, little did I realize that the valuable building blocks of my future professional life were laid with the extensive training and experience of the coatings industry at the R&D center in Mumbai of this paint major.

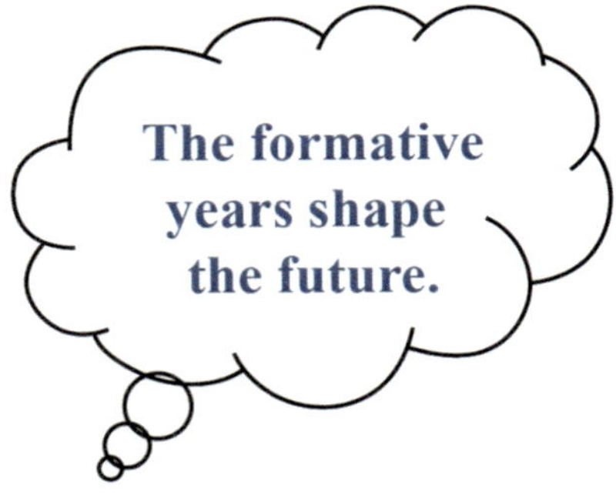

Life in the Laboratory

In early 1990, I started my first full-time role as a junior R&D chemist. It turned out to be a unique experience as this was a start of my professional life in true sense!

I gathered valuable experience and learning in the five years I was with this great company, and in this tenure, little did I realize that the initial hard work would secure my future job offers and my entire professional life, along with the financial security for the family.

The experience opened the door to the insights of coating technology in the paints and ink field, and during this period I befriended a lot of colleagues who remain my friends.

I was assigned the Decorative Paints section during my probation period to formulate various paints for home use, such as distempers, emulsion paints, and enamels for both interior and exterior applications.

The laboratory was headed by a veteran manager who was a great person with a meticulous approach toward work and discipline, along with strict expectations on goals and KPIs for his staff.

Once I was initiated in my job, I was assigned to two senior colleagues who were my mentors and imparted the nuances and explained the intricacies of the role as a chemist.

As any relationship starts with some hiccups, initial hesitation, and due to lack of confidence, I committed some silly errors at the job due to my relative inexperience, which became an object of ridicule and introspection for me.

So let me narrate a few encounters in detail.

As an initial task, I was assigned to process on a laboratory scale a paint and test its critical parameters for the finished product.

The paint during those times was processed with an equipment called the ball mill, which is operated by placing the grinding media in the form of ceramic balls to grind the main components of the paint, such as pigments, resins, additives, etc. to homogenize them.

This ball mill is then placed on a roller operated by electricity overnight to complete the dispersion of the pigment, and the fine dispersion is then measured on an instrument called a Hegmann gauge to check the completion of the process.

Due to my bad luck, I had forgotten to add the **grinding media in the ball mill,** and after overnight rolling, the correct finish of the paint could not be achieved.

My superior was surprised and came to inspect the experiment and identify the problem, which he noticed immediately and stated, *"Mr. Arte you forgot to add the grinding media," and without them even after a year, you cannot achieve the finish of the paint and complete the experiment!*

I realized my inadvertent mistake, took the experience in right stride, and started a taking deep interest in my job. Perhaps an initial setback always helps you to introspect and undertake course correction, as failure remains the best teacher.

Realizing my dedication and hard work, new responsibilities were added to my profile, and I was nominated for extensive trainings from the department.

I got enrolled for a diploma in paint technology at the Department of Chemical Technology Mumbai, a prestigious institute sponsored by my employer.

I studied at the academy for a year, attending classes after the working hours, and secured the third rank in the exam and received a cash prize of INR 100.0, which seemed meager now but was quite decent in the old times as a token of appreciation from the institute.

This success catapulted my confidence to a higher level after the initial setbacks at the start of my career as a R&D chemist.

As time progressed, I was transferred to the analytical laboratory for the testing of raw materials in coating technology.

A new change ushered in with the acclimatization of analytical instruments like gas chromatography, infrared and UV-ultraviolet, IR—Infrared and DSC—differential scanning colorimeter, which remain critical instruments in testing raw materials for any scientific investigation.

This remained a unique experience under the tutelage of Mr. K, a hands-on manager and a true leader with whom I hit off very well.

As days passed, I realized my peers started migrating for better career and economic prospects around the world. The Middle East felt very promising as an option to explore, due to the booming economies and opportunities it offered.

I decided to move on but cannot forget to acknowledge the immense contribution my employer had in my life, even till this date. I started my family, getting married, followed by the arrival of our son Aditya, which increased my responsibilities and made me take life more seriously.

Middle East incidentally offered me two job options, which were shortlisted after scrutiny to apply for.

a) With a FMCG multinational in the laboratory in Saudi Arabia.

b) Techno commercial opportunity with a leading trading house in Dubai.

Since my previous experience aligned perfectly with the opportunity in Saudi Arabia, however, I applied and chose the latter one.

As part of normal human psychology, we often tend to remain in our comfort zones, silos, and deal with what we know best, but this approach often limits us in unlocking our true potential.

So, once we move out of our comfort zone, we enlarge our perspective toward life, career, and our learning curve.

No risks No
gains!

Salesman by Chance

This chapter covers the period of exploring new opportunities outside my comfort zone and known environment in a foreign land of dreams – Dubai, United Arab Emirates.

I remember getting interviewed in the mid-nineties in one of the iconic hotels in Mumbai, The Taj.

The role envisaged was to set up a testing laboratory by offering technical service for the coating customers in the UAE with a very renowned trading house.

The interview was conducted by the Head of Sales and my future manager who would then incidentally become my first boss in Sales.

I would now state in retrospection that he was the first person to prepare me for the role of sales representative. He was a person having excellent sales aptitude who had decades of experience in the industry from his time working in India.

The interview concluded successfully. I got a brief idea of life in Dubai along with a remuneration that appeared quite attractive with a good saving potential, especially with the exchange rate conversion of currency.

The job profile envisaged setting up a small raw material testing laboratory near the warehouse. I landed in Dubai in September 1995 after a goodbye from the family.

As the flight landed at Dubai Airport, I noticed the tall skyscrapers from the airplane and was mesmerized by the new city of domicile. Little did I imagine that this city of dreams, with its hospitality and vibrancy, would host me and my family again after a few years for at least two decades.

I was received by company staff and realized the dry weather, heat, and scorching sun after stepping out of the airport in the afternoon of mid-1995. This initial encounter imbibed in my mind about acclimatization and adapting to the climatic conditions in my incoming work life.

I was then ensconced to the comfortable housing accommodation of the company, shared by a few colleagues who were quite young and were excited to see a new face in the accommodation.

I started my new phase with an introduction to two colleagues who were given the responsibility to induct me with formal training on the company's expectations and visit clients for technical support.

One of the colleagues is now settled in North America as a successful businessman, was an ideal friend, and we started getting along well.

My initial KPIs involved setting up a laboratory to test critical raw materials as an add-on service which needed to be processed and test various parameters like UV resistance, hiding power, viscosity, etc.

The initial problem for me in my job was the mobility part, as I had a visa from Al Ain and getting a driving license needed me to practice driving lessons in the Emirate of where the employment visa is issued, that's Al Ain, literally 1.5 hours driving distance from Dubai. It was impractical, as in those days, practicing driving in another emirate was not encouraged, so I had to resort to shared taxis and public transport to visit clients.

However, my colleague had procured a driving license and was mobile with a car, but I could not depend on him forever, hence I started venturing out with the public transport. Unlike today in Dubai and in UAE, where many options like the metro and an efficient bus network across the emirates have made traveling very easy and convenient, as the public transportation network in those days was gearing up to meet the future needs.

So, to begin with, I had to plan my client's visit for technical service by getting a shared taxi and then getting dropped at a common stop in the Industrial Area.

But sometimes I had to walk in peak heat to visit a prospective or current clients for technical support and later for sales generation as a regular feature.

In the early days, staying in Sharjah and traveling to Dubai were quite easy, as the traffic in the mid-nineties was very smooth. It was a practice in earlier times of taking an afternoon break for lunch and resuming office at 4 till 7 pm or 8 pm.

I realized that procuring a driving license was like securing a Ph.D. as this improved your mobility and you were independent to move around with the company vehicle, but this remained a distant dream due to my visa from a different emirate.

As a few months passed, my boss informed me to start taking charge of sales, visiting the clients, and generating sales to justify my costs. He handed me a sales target and KPIs along with the collection of payments from clients.

As a technical person, this was quite new to me, as selling emerged as a new challenge along with the collection of over dues. I questioned my boss by stating, "Is collection of payments also my responsibility?" To which he responded as:

"NO SALES IS COMPLETE WITHOUT THE PAYMENT BACK INTO OUR COMPANY ACCOUNTS."

The statement was pragmatic and a critical lesson in sales. It was an eye opener for an accidental sales representative like me to realize that without the money back in the pocket, no sale is complete. This remained my motto for the future sales jobs and expeditions, and I take it very seriously in letter and spirit.

It became my regular routine in the sales process, and most of my clientele in the United Arab Emirates were from the paint and construction industry and my technical background helped me to forge long-lasting relationship rather than only a transactional encounter.

Commuting remained quite arduous without a vehicle, especially during summers, as while walking for a meeting I used to get drenched in sweat and perspiration with a parched throat and turn up at the reception of clients in a disarray. But this was the time when you realize being human is a boon.

Clients and good Samaritans like Mr. AL, Mr., PX or Eng. NM working in Al Ain was one of the best human beings I have encountered, and Eng. NM remains a client after many decades, and they would state prior to the start of the meeting that please relax, have some water, be comfortable, and cool down, and we can continue our meeting after a few minutes.

The list is unending, I would like to mention another person, Mr. DRD, also, an ex-employee of my company in India who was then the laboratory manager for a leading multinational paint producer, with whom I could strike an instant bond.

I remember working for a trial in the lab testing of the raw material at the factory on Sheikh Zayed Road.

Our association continued, especially with Mr. DRD, during my second stint in Dubai after a decade, which I will cover in a subsequent chapter.

The takeaway from such encounters made me realize that no matter in the commotion of the competitive negotiations, surviving the battle against your competition and a competitive world despite the challenges, the human spirit always triumphs and humanity emerges as the ultimate winner, as I could notice the human angle and consideration in a tough competitive world.

My customers and clientele represented various nationalities with cross-cultural backgrounds. I also befriended an important supplier, Dr. JK, from a major producer in the UK, who later invited me to the UK and France for technical training at the laboratories in France and the UK for raw materials for the coating and ink industry in the summer of 1996.

Apart from the technical training, I also visited London during the weekend and was mesmerized by the historical architecture and monuments. The fortnight of training was a great experience, and it imbibed the virtues of professionalism shown by the British and French people and their attitude toward work and life, which was an eye opener.

I could notice the subtle cultural differences between the countries across the English Isles, as I remember a luncheon with the French counterparts which was a prolonged affair. It was a full course meal comprising fresh mussels, a distinct feature of French hospitality, and needless to state, the mesmerizing memories of the French and English countryside are still etched in my memory.

A valuable lesson of life was learned during the travel, with an episode at Charles De Gaulle Airport traveling back to Dubai after the training in August 1996.

As a protocol, the traveler needs to contact the airline office to reconfirm the ticket, which I was unaware of, and when I arrived at the counter for boarding my flight, I was told by the young French employee of Air France that I could not board the plane as my ticket was not reconfirmed.

This irritated me, and I started arguing with her, stating that I had a valid ticket and it was my right to board the flight. As my money was almost exhausted at the end of a fortnight's stay in Europe, and I was losing hope of a return as carrying a credit card was a privilege in those times.

She coolly took some time and started working on her computer monitor, and uttered the following words:

"SIR, RELAX. EVERY PROBLEM HAS A SOLUTION."

I could manage to get you a seat as the flight was not full, so relax and enjoy the flight.

These words still resonate in my ears after many decades, and it's so true: If we look at life in its complete perspective, every problem has a solution.

After all these years, I can only state that we, as human nature make a mountain out of a molehill when a problem surfaces, but in fact, these issues get resolved with the passage of time, as time remains the best solution.

Another name which I was fortunate to come across during my job was that of the country representative of Specialty Chemical Company represented with an office in Sharjah and was headed by Mr. UJR.

I was deputed by the head of my company to meet with him and check if we could initiate business with the company with their range of products. Hence, I started initiating visits to Mr. UJR, but destiny and God had other plans which I did not realize that time. It was to be that after 10 years, I would be part of this company in the Middle East.

I still remember an incidence of customer complaint on a product which needed to be addressed in Al Alin. I requested Mr. UJR to pick me up due to my immobility and drive me to the client's premises for an amicable resolution.

In short, more than a formal management degree, a prerequisite at least in those times or in the past was the tenacity to survive in the most demanding profession of sales with a service-oriented attitude, problem-solving skills, with a technical background as an add-on to help one sustain the job demands.

As the days passed, I was entrusted with more responsibilities and started attending business exhibitions, representing my employer in Dubai. One such example was the Middle East Coating show which holds a great emotional experience for me as I started attending, representing the company at the trade booth, and gathering the skills required for securing business contacts and networking.

In fact, the market and your clients remain the best teachers and mentors to guide you in the conundrum of complexities, as the Darwinian theory of survival of the fittest gets more prominence by embracing adaptability.

The experience with my Dubai employer, for which I will always remain indebted, enabled me to polish my skills from an introvert to an outgoing competitive Sales professional.

I also enrolled in a driving school as my visa got shifted to another emirate, which made attending driving lessons much easier. I cleared the initial hurdles of parking and other tests to initiate training on the road and attended two tests on the road, but failed and started practicing more vigorously to secure the license.

Life remained good in the company of colleagues, but the pinch of being from the family and a young, growing child made me home sick.

I would do an injustice if I do not mention a great colleague, friend, and a philosopher, Mr. MJS. A very humble person with great family values and an excellent sales professional with impeccable communication skills, great market intelligence acumen, and work ethics. I could learn a

lot from him during my first Dubai stint, and we kept the friendship of many decades till date.

After 18 months, I took a break and went back home and could realize my family missed me and my mother's Parkinson's syndrome was at an advanced stage. We were financially comfortable with the savings from the current job.

Post 36 months of service, I resigned and returned home to start a new struggle of securing a job back home in Mumbai.

Back in India

After the decision of leaving Dubai due to a compulsions back home, I landed back in Mumbai.

Life was back to square one as I had practically no job in hand in February 1998, and in the hindsight, when I look at it, the decision seemed irrational, but all's well that ends well!

I would state that the networking skills I had polished helped me in my desperate times during the pursuit of a job. As I remember during the early February 1997, I had attended the Middle East coating show and had a chance encounter with my ex-colleague from India, Mr. RKK, who was then the Technical Director for a major construction chemical player and he was attending the show with the MD of the company.

After exchanging greetings and visiting cards, I informed them that I would be back in Mumbai and meet them for prospects.

On landing back, I waited for more than three months for an interview call and started following desperately to get back into the industry. Here was an important lesson I learned about the term **"YOUR NET WORTH IS YOUR NETWORK,"** as this really helped.

I got selected for the job as Western India Sales Executive, reporting directly to the MD with a team of sales representatives to handle and streamline the channel partners, that is the distributors and agents of the company.

The job was paying me well; however, it was no way near to the saving potential that I had in Dubai and was sufficient to run my home and save a few dimes at the end of the month.

My new phase started, and I worked with the company for almost two years and would state proudly that the phase of working with the company was the best phase of my professional life.

During this stint, I realized that irrespective of the position one holds and the emoluments you receive, it's the satisfaction of the job and the experience you gain that help you to grow. This was undeniably one of the best companies I worked for, especially since it gave me the opportunity to directly report to the MD/owner of the company.

The main KPIs of my new job were to appoint new channel partners, and during this period I had to travel extensively across India. I had to conduct customer seminars and product introduction with various private and public institutions, meeting decision makers, consultants, and contractors, which was enriching my growth path.

I remember the arduous journeys by trains, bus coaches, and occasionally by flights to remote corners of a semi-continent India. Like, on the eastern border for conducting symposium on water proofing chemicals in a town called Siliguri for Eastern Railways, as this was a great traveling experience.

A travel to Chandigarh with a colleague on the historic Grant Trunk Road from Delhi at night in the winter, with mercury dipping very low, was another memorable moment.

This experience really helped me grow in sales and one of the best achievements in the company was managing to secure the biggest sales order with some background work, market intelligence, and hard work to secure an order of apply supply contract for water proofing chemicals. This was quite huge in terms of turnover in 1998.

The contract was for a newly built five-star hotel coming up near the Mumbai airport. It was being designed by a famous architect of Mumbai and constructed by a British contractor and a Chief Resident Engineer who came from the UK and set up his team.

I cannot recollect his name, but he was the main decision-maker and was assisted by his quantity surveyor, Mr. AS, who was responsible to scrutinize the technical aspects of products proposed for qualification.

During this crucial stage, I befriended Mr. AS who emerged as my coach and navigated me on the main competitors in the field, like the major multinationals, along with the product specifications and provided crucial market intelligence to pitch our value proposition.

I will narrate the process of handling a prospect scientifically in further chapters with a philosophy called customer competency.

The road to final negotiation was already laid with the meeting attended by our MD, who concluded the final agreement.

I recollect our internal discussion on the project by pondering and preparing all aspects of the negotiation phase, like **BATNA** (Best Alternative to a Negotiated Agreement), **ZOPA** (Zone of Possible Agreement) in terms of our final offer and **CNA** (Consequences of No Agreement).

This was the first biggest order in the history of the company and my efforts were well appreciated, but sometimes in the life of a sales representative, you may also remain an unsung hero and need to take both adulation and criticism in the right stride.

The success proved a booster shot for an accidental sales representative like me, as **nothing succeeds like success.**

Soon my options in the company became limited, which motivated me to search further new options in my career graph. While tendering the resignation, I became quite emotional with the MD, who stated that **the doors of the company are always open if I rethink to join again, which was a great testimony to my work.**

I then landed in new job with the regular process of interviews and group discussions in a multinational paint company in India and was appointed the Marketing and Sales Executive for Western Region Sales with the strong brand and had a team of three sales representatives as my direct reports.

The job was quite highly paid, but with high pay augurs high pressure and stress as the multinational paint company was competing with local entrenched giants, and it remained a David vs Goliath contest in the marketplace.

The pressure remained quite high, and my boss, the regional sales manager turned out to be very demanding and not patient enough to understand the overall situation and issues of working in an extremely competitive market like western India.

Soon, the heavy work pressure started affecting my work-life balance, as I did not enjoy my work anymore.

It was time to leave, and the Middle East started beckoning me again!

As once a Middle Eastern remains always a Middle Eastern. So, in mid-August, I applied for a job in Muscat, Sultanate of Oman, for a sales executive position with a regional building materials company, which represented the paint major with whom I worked in India in Oman. My candidature was a perfect business fit for my new employer.

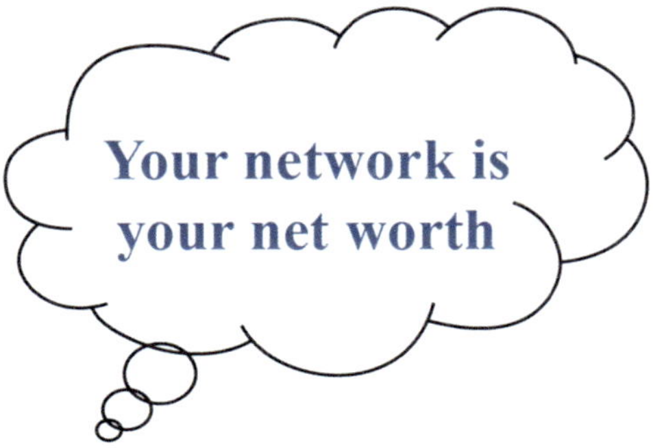

Sultanate of Oman

Oman remains one of the important milestones of my life in the profession of selling from 2000–2006.

The Sultanate of Oman is often referred to as one of the top tourist destinations of Gulf, and it's not an exaggeration as the country is very rich and diverse in its beauty, scenery, landscapes, architecture, and with its heritage preserved assiduously.

The best part of Oman which I noticed all along was the discipline as a nation, keeping the cities, towns, and hamlets spotlessly clean across, with greenery and plantations, hence culturally blending with modernity and tradition, and its architecture remains a cynosure to the eye.

An example to quote is the Royal Oman Opera House, an imposing monument in Muscat which was inaugurated a few years ago and blends Omani architecture with modernity as a unique amalgamation of ideas and creativity.

My journey began with Oman in September 2000, after I decided to quit the multinational paint player and applied for the job through a newsprint advertisement.

I was interviewed in Mumbai by the Deputy General Manager of the company, who after an exhaustive interview in Mumbai offered the job, which fitted perfectly as the Company, a building material giant, represented the paint multinational in Muscat and the position represented handling sales in the country.

The group was owned by one of the leading Industrialists of Oman which has diversified interests.

I needed to move out of Mumbai, and the Middle East was beckoning me again, so I accepted the offer and had to resume the duty, and after a few months, my family would join me in Muscat, which was my precondition for an offer.

The company provided a comfortable accommodation with medical facilities and other benefits. It offered an impression of playing by the rules and regulations to foster employee and employer relationship. I also noticed that many of the staff members were with the company serving for long, almost 20–25 years.

I was offered the position as a Sales Executive in the hardware division of the company catering to the construction industry and had a huge, diversified portfolio, warehouses, and branches across the country.

Working in Oman brought many firsts like securing the driving license, driving the first car in the Middle East, bringing my family to experience life outside India and last but not least, polishing and honing my selling skills.

Oman offered me the ubiquitous opportunity to service many products to the biggest luminaries of the country like the ex-minister, higher authority in police department, and a high-ranking official, which helped honing my skills in negotiation, which by far wouldn't have been possible without my stint in Oman.

A unique credential I proudly possess as a badge of honor in my selling life is the experience which I will narrate in the subsequent chapter.

I landed in mid-September in Muscat at Seeb International Airport and was chaperoned by an employee who brought me to the bachelor's accommodation to begin with till my family joined me after a few months.

Now the new challenge in Muscat began, and I resumed duty the next morning with an introduction by the DGM, who would then stay only for a few more months in the company after a long stint as he had plans moving to the UAE with a new offer.

I was introduced to my immediate colleague in the department, a veteran in the company, and with techno commercial selling of Auto Refinish paints.

Our clientele were major auto workshops or body shops of various car auto majors which did the touch-ups of cars with paint after the car got dented and needed repairs.

The agencies of multinational automobile giants were a few of our clients in the organized sector, followed by a host of unorganized private garages to cater to.

I was introduced to Mr. DSD, an ex-employee of my present company, who was then a resident representative of the company we were representing in Oman.

DSD was an amicable person to be associated with, and one of the best traits I could inculcate was his extensive network with clients and people across the board.

He could easily mingle and meander with the decision-maker of the account and any worker in the Bodyshop with great ease, cutting across the barriers of hierarchy and position and remaining humble, which I try to emulate in my professional life till date.

The KPIs were handed over to me with the team, comprising of MN and the color matching colleagues in our paint shop, to manage.

I enrolled in the driving school for the driving license and started the lessons. Meanwhile, I befriended with SS who was joining the chemical division as a manager. He is an amicable personality who remains our family friend till date. The other good friends I made were PJS, a colleague working for the another division of the company, and IRK, working in the HQ in Ruwi.

We instantly clicked as a quartet and formed a support structure, thus spending time together during weekends.

Oman was the first country which offered me to possess a car, albeit a company car after failing five driving tests and securing a driving license after 2 to 3 months of enrolling in the private driving institute with an Omani instructor. Securing the driving license was a great boon and a necessity which paved the way for my mobility to meet and visit customers on a regular basis.

During the interim period, my immediate colleague remained a support structure, driving me around which I remain indebted as a colleague, and later, we remained good family friends.

Once the driving license was procured, I got the company car for traveling across Muscat to Seeb, Mawelah, Barka, Nizwa, Rustaq, Sohar, and Sur, few of the cities, for meeting clients and beginning my family life phase in Oman.

The car offered was quite a good brand, but after a year and a half the aircon became quite faulty and was quite unbearable to travel in peak summers, despite repairing it many times.

I recollect an incidence when I asked my then Manager GVSG to accompany me for a client meeting, and he jokingly refused, stating it's better to travel in his car than get roasted in the journey, and then onwards used to drive his car for important client meetings with all humility.

My ordeal and my love story with my first car ended as the company offered me a new scheme to replace the car with a newly acquired agency of a Japanese auto giant by the group company.

Once my first car was allocated, I decided to bring my family to Muscat, which was in February 2001.

I was allocated a single-bedroom, fully furnished apartment in Ruwi near the office on company property with all amenities available in the neighborhood.

It especially made it easier for my wife to run errands on her own with supermarkets in the neighborhood and proved quite convenient before the advent of Amazon and e-commerce hit the world by storm.

In the interim period of four to five months, my contact with the family remained via telephone on a weekly basis, emails and letters, so once the family visa was secured, they packed the bags and embarked on a new stint in Muscat, and our son Aditya, who was barely five years old, was traveling for the first time by plane to embark on a new life in the Middle East and Oman.

A dream was realized as I started driving to the airport during the sunset to receive my wife and son at the airport and as they emerged after emigration, sounding a bit tense due to the new environment. We were all excited as we were reuniting after five months as a family.

The first weekend was celebrated by my close friends, offering us a family dinner at a restaurant in Muscat.

The house was well set, and we were almost settled.

I continued selling in my job with the refinish paint portfolio, and then our GM, a great leader and an engineer by profession, but began his career in our company by selling rebars for construction and always stated that as a salesperson we should sell almost anything available under the roof as selling remains a knack which needs to be regularly polished.

After 16 months, our GM decided to move me from the auto paints section to the hardware section, move me out of my comfort zone, and align me with a veteran manager.

A move and a decision imposed on me made me unhappy as my core competency remained in the paints and coating Industry. Now, I was entrusted to handle contractors, architects, consultants and government authorities with a portfolio of GI pipes, fittings, tiles, and sanitary ware to hone my selling skills.

After all these years, I realize how important it is to move out of your comfort zone and handle new challenges, as it made me a complete sales-oriented person, selling from all A–Z products under one roof.

From a specialty portfolio, I moved to a commoditized portfolio for a B2C clientele. Slowly, I started to take interest despite making errors in my judgment and moved away from the alignment and expectations of the veteran manager for almost 20 years in the division.

Soon I was aligned with another manager, who was a novice in hardware division replaced from another division, seemed totally confused to lead the team, and was dependent on the veteran salesperson of the team, Mr. P, for advice.

In hindsight, I could understand the philosophy of our general manager of bringing disruption to bring out the best in the employees, which was his mercurial trait.

Finally, after a few years in 2003, my prayers were answered with the arrival of GVSG. It felt like a new and fresh breeze coming in, as he was hailing from a multinational joining the hardware division in our company. This shift proved good for me, as GVSG was a complete man manager with a managerial style of consensus but also placing his points strongly and reminding colleagues on their lacunae with constructive feedback.

Our association lasted for 2.5 years, and he remained one of the best managers I had in Oman.

As I encountered some of the worst personalities mentioned as exceptions, but was fortunate as the list of good people was unending whom I could associate with in Oman, and probably my good karma played a major part in it.

GVSG

GVSG joining the company was "like a cool breeze blowing around comforting you in the summer desert" around a chaotic environment, as the earlier supervisors were quite orthodox in their managerial approach and here comes a fresh person to give a new lease of life to the situation.

I was almost driven to depression with the high work pressure and load for achieving the set KPIs.

The advent of GVSG on the horizon brought a sense of resistance from his other colleagues, as he almost broke the taboos of managing people by treating colleagues with respect and equality. Breaking the barriers of hierarchy and class remained a hallmark of his skills.

Slowly, he became more involved by guiding me in the day-to-day business of our hardware division, and soon I also developed a family relationship with him.

As the days passed, he offered me constructive feedback to improve my selling skills and excel in the job.

GVSG remained the first manager in my career to offer me a promotion in 2004 after recognizing my hard work and efforts.

Over a period, we expanded the business, and due to his entrepreneurial and risk-taking skills, we brought new principals or business agencies into our fold.

One such example was a chemical company from Kuwait. The decision was pragmatic and proved to be a good experience.

Let me now narrate a few incidences as highlights of my selling days in Oman.

The first decision was opening a showroom below the office, which displayed all the hardware items, from paints, tiles, sanitary ware, and fittings, etc. I was deputed to attend the clients nearing the evening hours and the walk-in customers.

These customers were from all walks of life in Oman and observing them along with their body language, facial expressions, and eye movements taught me to judge a serious or casual customer, an experience which would prove immensely valuable in the future.

My stint as a show room salesperson in the evening deputed by GVSG proved a milestone in my selling career as many luminaries, consultants, and decision makers from government department visited our showroom as the brand image of our company was towering in the psyche of clients, correlating it with quality and value for money.

The after-sales service and complaints were handled very professionally, which resulted in the company getting evolved to become a goliath and an economic powerhouse in the country with their well-diversified business interest and investments.

One of the personalities I was fortunate to be associated was the then ex-minister of the country. The gentleman was a senior person with an age above 60 and used to walk into our showroom frequently in the evenings along with his friend and associate without much fanfare or showing off his position of power by maintaining a low profile.

The ex-minister came across as a wise man with knowledge and experience. Our Omani colleagues briefed me about his status while I started attending to him as a client.

The ex-minister was there to purchase our products for his property. He was walking around and negotiating very hard for his requirements for paint, sanitary ware, and tiles.

This gave me an insight of the consumer psychology and the buying philosophy; despite the hierarchical position, everyone expects a better deal and value for money.

During the times his son was introduced to me, who owned a contracting company in Ghala Industrial Area. I used to visit his office to secure orders for GI pipes, tiles, and paints. I consider myself lucky for the opportunity to sell to two generations. The relation further grew above the buyer-and-seller relationship to a level of mutual trust and respect.

Another personality and government authority I was fortunate to attend to, was to a high-ranking police officer in Muscat. The police in Oman are called ROP (Royal Oman Police) and Colonel. A was responsible for the housing tenements, sports complexes, and offices of ROP and had the authority for approving various projects from budgetary allocation sanctioned by the government.

He remained a regular visitor to our showroom, and normally the sales representative, who was a veteran in sales and working with the products for many decades, would attend him. Obviously, he was most sought after by the clients, market, and even tutored many of our managers with his advice; nevertheless, he remained quite busy and sometimes not accessible to his regular clients due to the extreme workload.

Colonel. A was seeking my colleague for an important project and felt ignored by him. He called our divisional manager and sought another sales representative to attend to his immediate needs, wherein I was then sought out to attend to the immediate need of the prestigious client.

In hindsight, the lesson I learned was that no matter how busy a salesperson is in the day-to-day matters, a client should not feel neglected while he is seeking solutions to his immediate issues at hand.

I visited Colonel. A at his office. During the visit, he came up with a proposal suggesting proper sanitary ware, comprising of bath showers and taps, for the police barracks housing, the police staff, and new recruits in Muscat.

I saw this as a unique opportunity to promote a sturdy product for use at the hand of young officers in the residential barracks.

We had agencies of two suppliers, one with a long relationship with an Italian sanitary ware company and a newly forged relationship with a premium Indian sanitary ware brand.

The regional GCC team of our Indian principals, headed by Mr. AB, visited us in Muscat from Dubai to forge a new partnership, and GVSG motivated me to try and establish this brand in the market.

I took it as a personal challenge to introduce the brand in Oman within our portfolio, as the market remained flooded with Italian, German, Spanish, and English brands which had a ready receptive edge from clients, approving consultants, and project heads.

I took the two samples of a heavy-duty brass taps and carried them to the office of Colonel. A and as the saying goes, *"**The proof of pudding is in its eating,**"* as after holding the taps he got convinced and requested his other colleagues to look at the product, which after consensus got approved.

The taps from India were the right value proposition, and the icing on the cake was their competitive pricing. He immediately sanctioned the approval order and directed me to seek the order post-negotiation with the commercial department of ROP.

I was elated and immediately drove back to the office. In the back yard after parking the car, I noticed GVSG and waved the approval letter for the Indian manufacturer by the Omani authority for a project and mentioned we have done it.

With this achievement, my other colleagues also got encouraged to offer a sturdy, cost-effective product for customer needs.

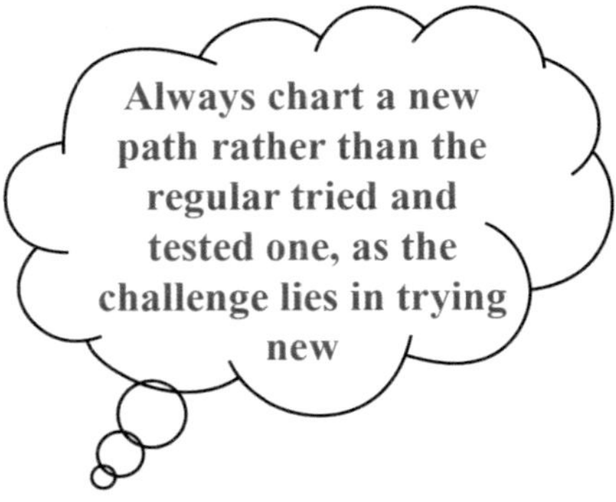

Another experience which I gathered and can describe as the zenith of my selling experience was securing a project and an order for sanitary tiles by attending the final negotiation with none other than one of the high-ranking personalities of Oman.

The project was shaping up well in a residential complex in Ruwi and was managed by our client, headed by Eng. JK as the project head of the contracting company.

I was deputed to attend to Eng. JK and suggest a few patterns, which got approved by the client. Then came the final negotiation part with the Sheikh.

Unfortunately, I could not understand the rationale of GVSG deputing me to lead the negotiation and avoiding it, but perhaps he wanted me to face the negotiations head-on.

I arrived at the appropriate time in a porta cabin at the project site, and there emerged a six-foot tall gentleman along with Eng. JK, who after the pleasantries questioned me, "Young man do you know me?"

I responded by stating, "Yes sir." I am briefed already and how can I help you now? …The Sheikh responded that we have approved the tiles for the project and need the final discount on the package, which ran into a few thousands in currency Omani Riyals.

I stated politely in the negotiation that I have the final mandate and no further discount emerged, so if required, your Excellency can call our head/owner of the company for closing the deal, and politely left the office.

Immediately, a phone call was made by the Sheikh to speak with the owner of our company, who refused a further discount, stating the price offered was competitive and stated that I empower my staff to take an independent decision.

Next week we received a call stating that our offer was approved, and we can start delivering the tiles.

Hurray… what else can I state further on this great success and negotiation as we remain fixed with our position to offer the best price without deviating further.

Engineer Z.

During the selling times in Oman, I specifically need to narrate an incidence about the true spirit of humanity and the wonderful humans I encountered on my journey.

The project I wish to mention was Sports Complex Nizwa and I was aligned earlier with GVSG's predecessor as my direct manager.

We got the sanitary tiles approved by the consultant, which was a pattern of beige color for the walls and light gray antiskid for the floors of the bathrooms. The approved tiles with the signature of the approving authority were then kept in the mock-up room at the site.

Once we received the order and the purchase order from the contractor, I had to fill in the requisition and give instructions to the warehouse, and then the goods were delivered to the site as a standard operating procedure.

After a few months, I received a call from the contracting company as the site engineer got summoned by the sports authority of Oman, stating wrong tiles were delivered at the site and we need to remove the tiles as we had been supplied white tiles, which were not acceptable.

The herculean problem now emerging was that with the rejection by the Sports Ministry Engineer, we were in deep trouble, as this was a human error on my part. I had mentioned the wrong code number in my requisition to the warehouse, and the only solution remained was to meet Engineer Z, a local Omani in charge of the project.

The site engineer of the contracting company was almost in tears as the threat of sacking from the company due to my mistake loomed large, as *"Success has many fathers and failure is an orphan,"* apart from the financial consequences we needed to face due to the human error.

We aligned a meeting at the sports ministry and along with the site engineer, I walked into the office of Engineer Z, who was a middle-aged man. It was early morning, and we pleaded our mistake and sought clemency, as this would turn out a huge financial cost of replacing the tiles due to a human error.

God answers your prayers when you need him the most, as the Engineer looked at us despite his busy schedule, and after a few minutes, he mentioned, *"Yalla approved for now, but do not commit such a mistake again."* That translates as let's go.

We stepped out of the office of Eng. Z, and we hugged each other with tears rolling from our cheeks, as an ordeal was coming to an end, and till date, I can only bless my benefactor and a good Samaritan who taught me that mercy is more pivotal than punishments for mistakes, which can be condoned.

Life in Muscat

I would slightly transgress from the topic and like to highlight about the lovely phase we had in Oman, spending more than five years.

Our lives and society remained closely knit, and socializing was a norm on weekends, especially when an extra half day was introduced in Oman.

Cherishing birthdays, and arranging send-offs to colleagues leaving for good kept us busy and active.

During those times, we witnessed one of the architectural wonders taking shape and finally getting inaugurated – the Sultan Qaboos Mosque, a must-visit and a touristic attraction of Oman.

As the years passed, I started planning for the next change, as my options remained quite limited for further growth.

In the interim period, one of the orders termed as a significant milestone that we secured with me playing an instrumental role was for the new, under construction Refinery at the port. It was of providing sealants for the concrete joints for the culverts to carry water.

We had entered into an agreement with a leading construction chemical player in Kuwait, representing them in Oman, and incidentally, as the saying goes, 'The world is small.' My ex-colleague from India named TK was the technical manager in the company.

Another ex-colleague, MK, was the assistant technical manager at the company in Kuwait, so relationship building with the principal was quite speedy. The sales manager of the company in Kuwait was the key player to approach us with the agency, which made a perfect business fit between the companies.

Initially, the business development task was offered to me based on my earlier experience of working with Construction Chemicals by GVSG.

I remember I was deputed for a week of training with the Construction Chemicals player in Kuwait. We planned it during the winter, the experience of which I cherished the most. I was taken care during the technical training by both my ex-colleagues with the evening sight-seeing tour of Kuwait.

They also awarded a certificate of training on the conclusion of the trip, which remains my proud possession, but little did I realize that I would again visit Kuwait and the company in my future job for selling our specialty chemical products.

The contract at Sohar port was awarded to a construction giant of the Middle East, and the project manager was Mr. D, who had earlier worked in Kuwait with the products of Kuwaiti Construction Chemical Player.

Initially, I had to interact with Project EPC coordinator, Mrs. RK, in the office in Muscat for sampling and approvals. We finally received the approval for providing the sealants, which comprised of almost 4–5 FCLs, which was a big achievement of selling a product beyond your comfort zone.

This was achieved by an excellent teamwork and the GM of our principal company flying into Muscat to assist us and by far remains another selling milestone.

Soon the time for change began, and I would like to emphasize how your past relationships and connections help you in securing the next job and can only state that a great teamwork is a dream work.

I received a call from none other than from MJS from Dubai, who had received the offer to join a global chemical player as a regional sales manager, but he was not interested and recommended me as the person fitting the bill.

MJS informed me that I should apply for the job, and this was a great opportunity to seek a change.

I need to acknowledge and mention the role of the then executive assistant of the company for checking with me if I can fly to Dubai for an interview. This was an impossible task, and I was candidly informed about the problem. So, as an alternative, she requested the Managing Director to drive to Sohar, Oman near the UAE border, which is an hour and a half drive from Dubai, and me joining them from Muscat to meet me for a preliminary interview.

I informed the GVSG in Oman about this move, who wished me all the best. I was interviewed by Mr. SKR, the then Managing Director of the company, and by Mr. UK, my colleague who came to interview me at Sohar, and I cleared the first step successfully.

The final interview was conducted within 30 days' post interviewing a few candidates in Dubai. The then Vice President of Sales of the Business line flew down from Germany along with the MD and drove again to Sohar for the final selection. The interview was very smooth, wherein I successfully answered the questions posed by the Vice President of Sales.

One of the questions posed to me during the interview was, how does a company lose its share in the market? I answered by stating that the loss of clients to competition, erosion of market share, and due to indifferent attitude of salespersons to the clients and their needs contribute to the erosion of market share of the company, which impressed my interviewers.

I received a confirmation from the MD in the evening, giving me an idea of my pay scale and emoluments and was asked how fast I could join the company, to which I stated I would need 60 days to wind up my affairs in Oman.

I disclosed my decision to GVSG, who was very happy for me and stated that he would ideally be happy if I were to continue in Oman, but since I received a great opportunity, he would help me in my next move.

Initially, my wife and son were quite reluctant to move again for a new change, and they opted to travel back to India, and so began my new journey to Dubai.

After saying goodbye to my friends, colleagues, and Oman which till date occupies a special corner in our heart as Oman as a country and the valuable experience I garnered in sales remains simply phenomenal.

Thank you, Oman. Shukran Oman.

No risks No gains!

New Phase in UAE

It was the end of August 2006, in peak summer, when I landed for the next challenge in Dubai, United Arab Emirates, with a direct flight from Muscat, Oman.

My family was back in India, waiting for the papers to join me once I settled into the new company.

It was a nostalgic and emotional moment for me as I was starting my second stint in the country after almost a decade in one of my favorite cities, Dubai, a modern megapolis which keeps changing regularly with its ambitions touching the limits.

The city remains a beacon of innovation, entrepreneurship, and risk-taking ability, which propels it and the country to the forefront of the global comity of nations.

In fact, this inherent quality of Dubai holds true for companies, individuals, marketing, and sales professionals to imbibe the high standards set by the rulers of the UAE to survive and grow exponentially in an extremely competitive environment and emerge tall during the various disruptions happening on a regular basis.

One notable change I need to mention, which I noticed after a decade, was the traffic between Sharjah and Dubai. It was quite natural as times progresses, a journey in 1995–1997 one could reach Deira from Al Wahda street in Sharjah in a few minutes, which in peak traffic now could take 40–60 minutes, depending on the destination.

I was immediately boarded in Crowne Plaza hotel Deira by my new employers till I could manage an accommodation and regularized my naturalization and residency status in the UAE.

I managed to connect with MJS, my ex-colleague and benefactor from my previous Dubai times, and reached my old office to meet my past colleagues. It was a very nostalgic moment for me personally to relive the old days.

August 2006 was the month of joining the new specialty chemicals company at its office. I reached the place at 8 a.m. sharp and recollect meeting our sales, IT, and other staff.

I was offered an introductory round of the office with our then Executive Assistant and my new benefactor, who was performing many roles as an Executive Assistant, HR, and Accountant for the company very meticulously and had been a part of the company for more than 10 years.

This was followed by the introduction with the new managing director.

An introduction with the other staff members and other colleagues was concluded, as the office in those times remained quite low on head count and was quite a close-knit family, unlike today, where the staff count has increased exponentially and keeps growing as times keep changing.

Soon, the handing over process of business commenced along with my colleague UK, which involved traveling to neighboring countries of Kuwait, Oman, Qatar, Bahrain, and Saudi Arabia to meet clients and distributors. I must state that it was a complete, meticulous, and professional handover like a mentor, as I could have expected, and made my task easier to step in.

My family soon joined me, and we managed an accommodation in Sharjah in the Qasimiya neighborhood and by sheer coincidence, in 1995, when I had started my first stint in the UAE, I was staying on the same street. So, you never know where luck can place you and end up revisiting your past or Karma!

I was introduced to my colleagues in Germany and was instructed to visit Germany in November 2006 for a product training and induction. I started my visa process to visit a new destination and country, Germany.

Germany

November 2006, during the peak winter season, which also turned out to be my first winter experience in Europe, I boarded a flight to Frankfurt with anxiety and curiosity to learn about my new employers, as I was employed to work for two business lines, and I experienced nervous palpitations in my heart to meet new faces and meet their expectations.

I had a planned stay of 15 days in Frankfurt and Dusseldorf, covering the cities and visiting the production sites located in the north and west of Germany.

My stay was arranged at the Maritim Hotel, a German chain of hotels on "Rhein Strasse" in the beautiful and historic city of Darmstadt. Mr. OA, my friend, philosopher, and guide, had the responsibility of training me on the technical part of our products.

In the morning, after savoring the traditional German breakfast, I arrived at the gate of the company, and after the security and visitor check, OA arrived at the gate as my host and trainer to receive me.

I noticed at first impression a well-built, rather rotund person with blue eyes and a charming personality in his late forty's approaching me with a handshake and pronouncing my name in a typical German way, stating: "I am OA, your colleague for the resin part of your portfolio," and handed me over the training itinerary.

I could notice his eyes were screening me like an X-ray machine, and for a second, I thought, *did I dress inappropriately*? But after many years of association with him I realize that he was reading my body language to gauge me as, the new colleague responsible for handling the Middle East territory.

Little did I realize that me and my family's association with OA would last and remain intact even after his retirement in 2017.

The training in Darmstadt lasted for a week, and I realized the importance of German corporate ethics and culture and its emphasis on improving the skills of employees by training them on a regular basis.

After nearing 16 plus years, I can proudly state that perhaps I am one of the most highly trained employees on the regional level, with trainings covering subjects like technical, marketing and sales, trade compliance, compliance, and many more to state.

Just recently in 2022, while I was attending the technical training virtually to refresh my product knowledge, our Applied Technology Head conducting the training questioned me by stating, " **Sachin, do you need training? you can as well conduct the training for other colleagues."**

I think this was a testimony of the time and resources invested by the company in me as an employee to ensure I have the right skill sets that remain effective in my job.

I am tempted to narrate a dialogue which was narrated by the trainer in one of the training institutes while attending a corporate training session highlighting the importance of training.

The dialogue was between a department manager and the CEO of a company, and the manager complained stating, "We invest a lot in training employees and after acquiring the desired skills they leave us."

The CEO astutely responded by stating, **"What if we don't train them and they stay?"**

During the training in Darmstadt, I managed to offer a positive impression to my Trainer and colleagues, and then proceeded to the next part of my training for the other part of my portfolio near Dusseldorf in the state of North Westphalia region of Germany.

The site was humungous, and the training was conducted by a few colleagues who have since retired, and my host was Mr. FEX, who recruited me for the job and offered me his expectations from the region.

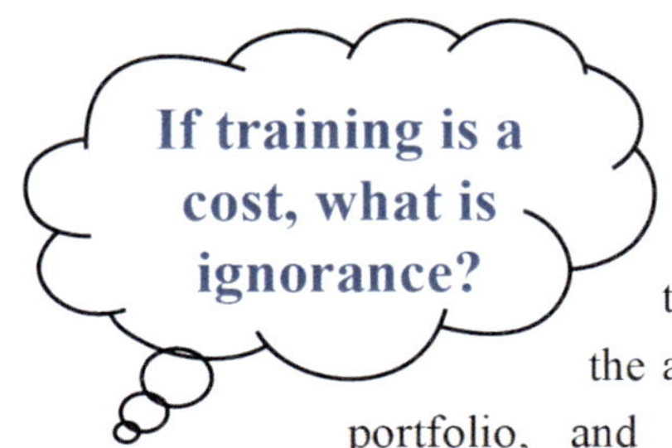

I noticed the comfort level of the colleagues imparting the training, as they were assured of my technical background and the ability to handle a complex portfolio, and after 15 great days in Germany, I was back boarding my flight to Dubai.

Traveling with OA

I need to narrate a few incidents while traveling in ME and Africa, during which I learned the basics of business development, sales management, and handling customer objections while traveling and meeting customers with OA.

Although a hardcore technical person in all his professional life, but had a lot to offer with his global experience, and those joint travel learnings still resonate all these years as my learning takeaways.

Somehow coincidently, our joint travels in the region, frequenting twice a year, always ended up with challenges due to various external factors, but we could conclude our trip successfully despite the hiccups, which are quite interesting to narrate below.

OA was the Global Technical Manager, and his prime responsibility was to offer technical service, recommendation, and travel around the globe to visit customers, and initiate business development by offering product recommendations of our portfolio. He started very early with the company in early twenties and retired with almost 40 years of vast experience.

During the training, I was assessed by him for my technical acumen, but due to the courtesy of my technical background, he found it easy to augment the training module, ultimately giving him a confidence of a suitable person to handle the territory after handover by my colleague.

The qualities which I could learn and apply in my job are narrated below, which can also be of help for many aspiring B2B sales professionals and new entrants in the profession.

a. **Screening the client** – Once a meeting got concluded with a client with a discussion and technical offering with its team.

OA would come out and conclude, prophesizing that we have 50.0 %, 75.0%, or 100.0 % chance of success in the account just after a brief encounter, and advise me to handle the opportunity diligently.

This is termed as understanding and reading the client with the neuro-analytical skills to ascertain the time to be invested in cultivating an account.

If the case was hopeless with the client, who was only interested in checking prices and comparing the offering, AO would simply state, **"Sachin, it's hopeless to invest time with the prospect..."**

After many years, I am still a work in progress to completely adapt to the skill of concluding the climax of a sales call and its result.

b. **Complete the actions immediately after the sales call** – OA remained a workaholic and a diligent employee, as he would post his reports immediately after the meetings in our system with conclusive actions and responsibilities aligned for action.

At any point of time, he utilized the time with maximum productivity at the airport lobby, late evenings, or even early mornings before meeting him in the hotel lobby for breakfast.

This habit was quite productive, as he could not lose track of the meeting and follow up on the opportunity offered.

c. **Peripheral vision** – OA had the divine god gift of using his peripheral vision while visiting and analyzing an account.

In the early days, the reception offered the situation of the customer just like an airport of any country offering the first impression on landing.

He had the unique knack by judging the punching muster of the employee attendance card and the dust accumulated on it by concluding about the account.

Does the company give due diligence to discipline, tidiness, and professionalism? Even the brochure stands at reception, and its clutter could help him conclude the situation at the account.

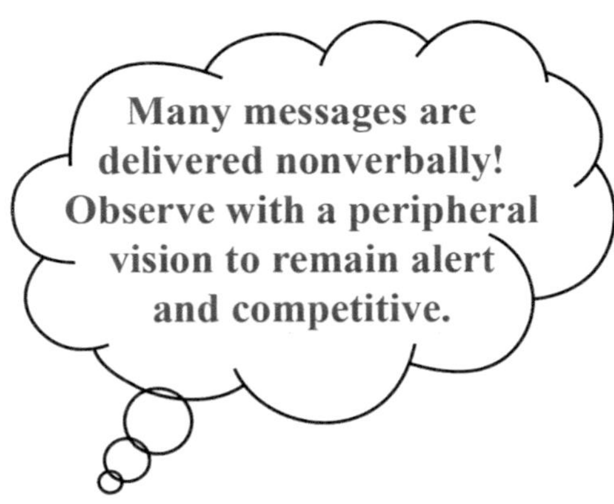

I would like to narrate some of the challenges we encountered in our joint expeditions in the region lasting for more than eight years.

It's always said that to know and judge a person or a country, one must travel to form an impression.

d. While we were traveling in Saudi Arabia in 2007 and visiting Jeddah, Riyadh, and Dammam for a week, we had a connecting flight to Muscat to cover our visit to Oman and conduct meetings with our clients and prospects.

In earlier times, a protocol prevailed with all airlines that the passenger should reconfirm the ticket for the further destination, and somehow, unknowingly, I forgot this necessity once again after the 1996 incident while traveling from Paris back to Dubai, which I had narrated earlier.

I was off-boarded due to the non-confirmation of the ticket, and OA had to continue his journey as reservations were made in advance. So, rather reluctantly, he agreed to continue the flight, as I stated that on the next day the appointments were fixed, and he could take a taxi to visit clients in my absence.

I then had to activate plan B by calling our travel agent and our office executive assistant, who could manage to book me a flight from Dammam to Abu Dhabi and then to Muscat so I could land in Muscat at 2.30 a.m. in the morning.

This plan worked, and I was at the breakfast table to meet OA, who got much relieved to see me join the rest of the trip successfully.

e. In 2008, now it was OA's turn, as we were covering Kuwait and had our connecting flight to another destination and country in the Middle East. Once we arrived at the check-in counter, it seemed OA could not board due to a certain visa technicality.

OA was naturally disappointed, and I had to conduct the remaining part of the trip to the destination, which remains one of my favorite cities.

f. On one occasion, we also spent almost seven hours in the queue for immigration after landing at 18.00 hrs. at the airport. The huge serpentine queues and the process was very slow, and we emerged out of the airport at 1.00 a.m. in the morning, checking in at the hotel, completely tired.

I jokingly referred to OA that by sheer coincidence, I must endure all such challenges only whilst traveling with him.

g) In one of the client meetings in Middle East, which was quite acrimonious with tempers running high, I was personally blamed for not taking corrective actions for product complaints causing huge issues with the final processed product as it started solidifying.

OA defended me, stating that Sachin does not have the mandate, and unless he visits the client to check the root cause and take conclusive call. In fact, Sachin was on vacation and was coordinating the efforts. He successfully defended our company and blamed the client for not being transparent to offer a general formulation and the ingredients employed by using our product, and resolved the issue amicably.

This incident proved him as a colleague who could stand with people and other colleagues and defend them during thick and thin!

One incidence which I would like to narrate and emphasize is about the concept of peripheral vision, which I inculcated from OA and successfully implemented in one of the travels.

In 2012, I had completed a course and was equipped as a certified practitioner of Neuro Linguistic Programming, which helps me even today to assess situations and adapt accordingly.

OA and I were traveling in 2012, catching a flight from Kuwait to Bahrain, and noticed a young man whose overall body language appeared to be tense, nervous, and uncomfortable at the check-in counter.

In the flight, which was quite empty, the person whom I was observing occupied the middle row next to our side row. I noticed the strange behavior continuing right from the check-in counter as the gentleman appeared more tense during the journey.

I asked OA if he could notice some unusual behavior, to which, at first, he stated he was not sure, but after a few minutes, he responded, "You are right Sachin!"

After a flight of 60 minutes plus, we were at the immigration and could notice the authorities asking the young man to step aside and was interrogated for verification.

Perhaps this man was hiding something or might be a wanted person.

This experience highlights we as individuals should remain alert and take non-verbal cues from people whom you casually or intentionally interact to assess.

The encounter whether in private or business life, this lesson holds true.

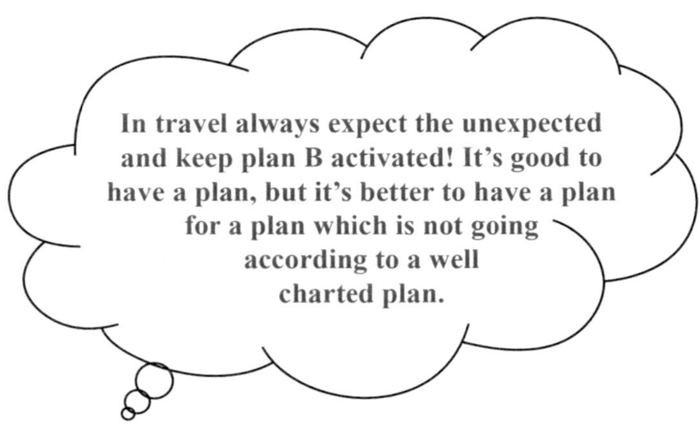

Man Management

I am a true believer of the paradigm that a company is not made up of its products, offerings, services, innovations, or their market reach but it's judged by the quality of its people!

It's not about products, but about people well-articulated below by the great American essayist.

"The true test of civilization is not the census, nor the size of cities, nor the crops, but the kind of citizen that the country turns out."

– Ralf Waldo Emerson

Does this not hold true for modern corporates and business empires?

I am fortunate to come across a great person in my life named Dr. KB, a polymer chemist from Mainz University, an ex-colleague, and a family friend who remains close to our hearts after many years of association, even after his departure to another company in 2018.

I must admit I have never encountered such a vibrant human being with full of zest toward work and life like KB.

In fact, he was one of the best man managers in my entire professional life to be associated with.

My first encounter with KB was in April 2007 in the historic city of Mainz in Germany, the city of Gutenberg, the inventor of the printing machine in an ecotel hotel hosting our sales meeting.

A bespectacled gentleman walked toward a rather shy and overwhelmed Sachin and introduced himself as the marketing manager of a product line I was handling in the past.

I casually informed him about the need to sample a few grades for a prospect in the UAE to which he responded, "Sachin, we will offer you as many bags as you desire as samples to support you!"

A truly magnanimous person, who always covered the extra mile to support the colleagues and staff in Sales with price, rebates, and technical support, and at times even swam against the tide to support his team.

As time flew, we both grew older, and our families connected well. The latest was his visit to Expo 2020 in early 2022 in Dubai with his wife and spending a memorable evening at our house. It has been since 2018 that KB has left the company as the portfolio was divested, but we continue our connection unabated.

KB, his wife, and their daughter remain excellent host, as I remember, whenever we finished our sales/training near Dusseldorf, KB always drove us with colleagues back to

Darmstadt, near Frankfurt, and invited us for an excellent dinner at his home overlooking the magnificent Rhine River.

Mrs. KB made it a point to cook spicy chicken curry with basmati rice to make me feel at home, and his entire extended family also started to know me well.

The highlight that I recollect was in 2018, while me and my wife were on vacation in Germany and stayed in his hometown. It was coincidentally Mrs. KB's birthday, which we were graciously invited to. The next day, KB arranged a guided city tour of historic Mainz and other nearby areas.

I miss KB on a regular basis in the business life, as he remained the best man manager and believed in empowering the salesperson to take independent decisions in the best interest of the business.

His passion for business remained exemplary. To give an example, he used to visit supermarkets while on the road to check packaging goods which used our products to feel the market dynamics.

During that period, our business grew well in the region with his support and involvement, as he was keen on supporting the business in a developing region to grow with additional rebates as a policy.

Unlike today, most of the management techniques in companies turn out to be micromanaging people, which is not a healthy practice in the long run as employee engagement starts eroding with the motivation levels even deteriorate.

Hence, if a sales representative needs to excel in the field, she/he must be reassured that they need to take independent decisions and be backed even in failure by the superior!

Well, that was KB for me!

Tracking Meetings and Encounters

Every prospect or client encounter as a thumb rule, needs to be well documented where the onus lies mostly on the sales representative. This habit is very productive, as we do not lose track of the development and follow up actions in an account.

I want to narrate an amazing example of this practice, which can prove very effective in the business development.

In 2008, I received a call from my colleague from Singapore, Dr. RD, for visiting Dubai to arrange client meetings, followed by attending the regional sales meeting and conduct a training for the participants from the region.

I arranged the itinerary for RD and took an appointment of a client in Dubai, who later became our key regional account for the business line.

The meeting was fixed with the decision maker, that's the CEO and technical advisor, with whom I had developed a good working relationship.

RD as a person is very sharp, well-organized, and meticulous in his conduct and goes into the details of any topic prior to arriving at a decision.

The meeting was at the Jebel Ali office of our client, and RD initiated the meeting with the presentation of our products as a value proposition to the client.

During the tea break, RD nudged me, stating that he is familiar with the technical advisor and remembered meeting him a few years back in India while presenting our products at a meeting with a paint producer in Mumbai.

I was amazed and surprised and countered him about how he recollected the face of the Technical Advisor, to which he stated that this personality was the most silent and observant one amongst the other vocal attendees at the meeting a few years back.

I was speechless as RD had recalled an encounter with a client which was quite old and could recollect it in verbatim. The habit is crucial to ensure the continuity of your proposition to a client or prospect and helps to keep track of your records.

Persistence Is the
Key for Success

A meticulous preparation followed with persistence for any eventuality remains a major factor for success or failure whether in business or to that matter in life.

We had introduced a new concept to the Middle East climatic topography, and it was planned to be demonstrated to the approving governmental authorities in UAE.

The product was a specialty which needed a machine for application.

Our local partner had planned an extensive media frenzy and involved a local event management company for covering the product trial.

Unfortunately, while the trial was conducted in full public view with government dignitaries attending the event on a summer evening at the road exit junction, we realized the demonstration did not generate the proper quality of result. The blame game started with our machine manufacturer blaming us for the quality of product produced with our raw materials, which was not the fact.

In fact, the machine used for the demonstration did not generate the desired result and was quite an embarrassing moment for all of us.

The trial from our part was attended by BKC, our then Sales and Marketing Head of the region, me and another colleague handling the technical department flew from Germany to conduct the trial, along with the machine technician traveling also from Germany.

Despite conducting many trial runs at our partner's backyard, we were quite prepared, but seems destiny had some other plans on the actual D-Day, that's on the date of the trial.

This setback almost aborted the introduction of the concept to the region, but we kept persisting toward our goal and emerged successful after a few attempts with the new concept for the region.

Since then, we never looked back as the new concept was accepted in the region as it offered a solution to a perennial problem. It was an excellent teamwork, which was further carried over successfully by another colleague once I left handling the portfolio to establish this concept and grow the business exponentially with his dedication.

So, in a nutshell, despite preparations, things can go wrong, but we should not deviate from our original goals and remain focused on the objective.

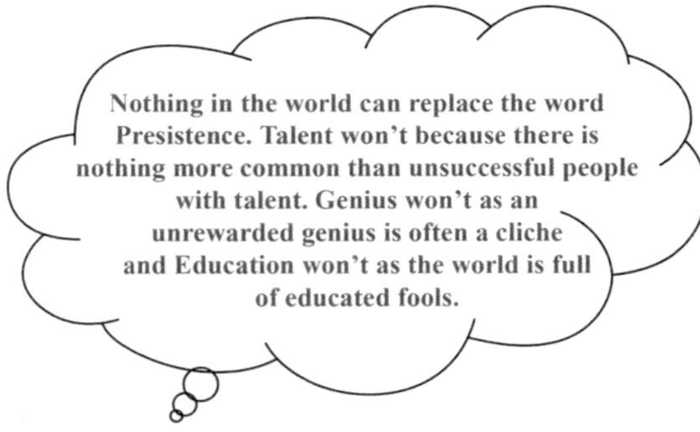

Sales Management Basics with My Conclusive Findings

No matter how many disruptions we as a human race will encounter in the future, we will remain adaptive and resilient.

The latest challenge the in form of Covid-19 heralded the introduction of hybrid work model and selling techniques; however, I remain a firm believer of the fact that nothing can replace the human interface F2F that's, face-to-face selling, and elucidate my argument as below.

- ✓ The face-to-face interaction always evokes spontaneous stimuli and responses, which is irreplaceable with the virtual calls.
- ✓ I can recall many virtual meetings, although a necessity in the pandemic period having to navigate with connectivity issues with reception and audio clarity, lag, and buffering.
- ✓ Immediate conclusion and actions can be drawn out from a F2F interaction.
- ✓ People with a visual and kinaesthetic affinity prefer face-to face meetings.

- ✓ You can deceive the world, but your eyes and body language cannot be deceptive for a smart negotiator to conclude/close the sale.
- ✓ Finally, a firm handshake evokes an immediate connection and trust.

Theories of Selling.

Let us first understand the theories of selling in order to understand sales management.

There are many theories of selling, but I would like to emphasize the most critical one below.

1. **AIDAS** – The acronym stands for Attention, Interest, Desire, Action, Satisfaction.
2. **Right set of circumstances theory.**
3. **Buying formula theory.**

I would now discuss the theories contextually.

AIDAS – This theory predominantly focuses on the role of the salesperson.

It starts with the initiation of **Attention** in the value proposition, be it the product, service, or about the company represented, followed by provoking the **Interest,** and then followed by evoking the **Desire.** Finally, the **Action,** like offering a sample, a trial, quote which culminates in **Satisfaction,** which is the experience/finale of the action which might also result in dissatisfaction and complaint.

Right set of Circumstances – The theory propounds the logic that all the circumstances were right leading to the closing of the sales.

For example, the market conditions, demand and supply, price, and service leading to the sale.

Buying Formula Theory – The theory fundamentally is heavily dependent on the buyer.

- It opines that the buyer's requirement is predominant in terms of closing the sale and places emphasis on the buyer's need and wants.

It emphasizes the needs or problems of the buyer and if the salesperson can assist the buyer in finding an appropriate solution to the problem, which is in the form of a product or service, it can end in deriving satisfactory sale result.

I personally feel that as a sales representative, the only part which is under control and can be contributed by the individual sales representative is the **"AIDAS"** part.

An individual cannot influence the circumstances, which remain beyond control, nor can the buyer's needs be influenced at a particular time.

So, keep practicing AIDAS and carry on, as only this part of the theory remains under the control of an individual as other factors remain elusive.

I personally practiced the theory across my selling life, which helped me emerge as an effective salesperson.

Navigating Through a Complex Account

Often, while we approach a new account it is quite important to conduct research via various tools on the actual mapping of an account.

I was fortunate to attend one of the trainings organized by my company, conducted by external trainers of the corporation specializing on mind mapping and on identifying the various stakeholders and handling a complex account.

A map of the account in my opinion are the stakeholders, founders, financial position of the account, its future vision and mission, the portfolio, and its overall industry competitiveness along with the industry trends.

In fact, this makes it easier for a salesperson to augment the strategy and submit the value proposition to the actual decision-maker.

There are various tools available to conduct the research and is also termed as **Customer proficiency** in understanding the account in its true spirit.

So, what is customer proficiency?

1. Understanding of the client beyond Google and metaphorically into blood, flesh, and bones that's in person.
2. Building sustainable, long-term relationships and not the transactional one with mutual trust and respect.
3. Value addition to the customer's needs and their perceived problem with an offer of a solution.
4. Forging win-win situations.
5. Breaking bread with customers as in Eurasian culture, which is not literally eating bread but developing and cultivating long-lasting friendship.
6. Building on the success to replicate with other accounts.

Let us first understand the various stakeholders in an account or in a prospective account.

Any account has five buying roles in every complex sales process: They are Economic buying influences, user buying influences, technical buying influences, and techno-commercial influence.

They are broadly classified as 1) Decision maker 2) Gatekeeper 3) Coach 4) Fence sitter 5) User.

The Decision Maker:

Role: Gives final approval to buy.

Focus: Effect on the decision on the organization.

Can control expenditure and release of funds and holds the right to **VETO.**

This role is executed normally by the CEO, departmental heads holding a higher position in the hierarchy.

The GateKeeper:

Role: Screen out various proposals and situation.

Focus: Match expectations.

Judge's solution and supplier.

Evaluates measurable and quantifiable aspects.

Uses the function as a specialist to navigate the decision.

Does not hold the final decision but can influence the VETO.

This role is normally performed by the buyer, R&D person, or even the receptionist in an account, blocking your efforts to meet the decision makers or coach in an account.

The Coach:

Role: Your success with the proposal.

Focus: How can we make this happen?

The primary aim of the sales representative is to identify and cultivate one good coach or even more, and not necessarily they are being a part of the buying company.

This role is normally performed by an external consultant working for the buying company or even by an influencer in the department like purchase, supply chain, R&D, or applied technology.

Fence Sitter:

Role: Acts as a bridge during the entire process with a wait and watch policy.

Focus: Primarily opportunistic and transactional – in an eventuality resulting in the success of any proposal, is ready to take the credit and, in failure, try to deflect the blame.

The primary aim of a sales representative is to identify such fence sitters, who typically are looking at other's shoulder for decision and are typically neutral in action; hence, try to convert them toward your side. The role is performed by assistants in Purchase, R&D, and Supply Chain who have a minor role in decision-making.

The User:

Role: Judges' impact on job performance.

Focus: How does this impact my performance?

Represents the demand from an operational point of view.

Considers the benefits/disadvantages of the offered solution.

Is often personally affected by the project.

The role, especially if we are in a specialty industry, is performed by the R&D chemist, the departmental user of the value proposition.

In a nutshell, some roles remain interchanging and dynamic, and it's the acumen of a professional salesperson to navigate through the conundrum of a complex account to avoid the gatekeepers, befriend a coach, and reach the decision maker.

Initially, I used to struggle to mind map an account and used to get frustrated because desired results remained elusive, but an overall experience helped me to create a map of an account to approach the final decision maker with a value proposition to succeed in the war of sales against competition.

In a nutshell, identify your hidden or discreet Allies, who are the people having a say in the overall decision making and can help move you forward. They can be your company admirer, a former colleague in the prospective account or even your former customer.

Virtue of Patience in Selling

I remain a firm believer of the word Patience, which can yield great dividends in life, be it professional or in private life.

Although in the instant two-minute noodle world, we all strive for fast results, perhaps this might be quite practical, but in the highly specialized B2B selling process, it remains quite time-consuming. Like in the case of the speciality chemicals business, as many stakeholders are involved in the decision-making process.

Any new development needs approval from the technical department, the commercial department, the approving governmental authorities, and the final consumer, so this remains a quagmire or labyrinth to navigate for a sales representative.

In fact, I feel tempted to mention the trait of a bird called a vulture waiting with patience for its prey or a lion in the African savannas waiting patiently for hours before leaping to go for the final kill are a few examples. I would like to advise to emulate these traits, but with a positive connotation.

I nostalgically remember my interaction with a reputed protective paint manufacturer in Saudi Arabia around 2010/2011 while on a visit and traveling with our local distributor. I checked with the colleague about the product portfolio it manufactures and was informed about a specialized paint which requires resins.

My colleague from the local distributor made a cold call to the purchasing and technical department soliciting the request to meet them and was immediately confirmed.

After we arrived at the gate, we waited in the reception for almost two hours, as we were informed by our hosts that they were quite busy.

I was losing my patience and prodded my distributor colleague to cancel the meeting, but managed to stay calm. Finally, we were called for a techno commercial discussion after a long waiting time in the reception.

After a preliminary meeting, we arrived at short listing of a few grades for sampling and commercial offer.

Luckily for me, my technical colleague in the field of specialized coatings, now long retired, assisted with all the guideline formulations, and samples and even visited the prospect along with me after a few months, and subsequently, we were informed about the technical approval of our resin.

We received the purchase order to supply a large quantity of the resin, a business which ran for two to three years till the company stopped producing the specialized paints.

Retrospectively, after all these years, I think if I had not waited for two hours at the reception of the company, the opportunity offered would not have materialized.

To summarize the most common qualities of a good salesperson can be many: ambition, appearance, business sense, courtesy, curiosity, integrity, knowledge, loyalty, motivation, originality, poise, friendliness, mental abilities, interest, self-control, self-starter, and clarity in speech.

However, the most important basic qualities are a) Empathy and 2) Persuasion.

Always try to place yourself in the shoes of the opposite person to understand their point of view and empathize on the client's situation rather than having a one-sided myopic view to secure and close the sales at the earliest, as this might prove a short-term rather than a long-term thinking, detrimental to the future.

Relationship Selling

The title of this chapter may sound misleading, so am I implying that I am initiating any relationship with the buyer?

Well, it's firmly a **NO.** But let's first understand what business is all about.

Management guru Peter Drucker stated that there is only one valid definition of business – to create and keep customers.

Companies are not in business to make things but to make customers!

The essence of keeping a customer is to stay in touch. Hence, in simple terms, we can state that marketing and sales encompass activities like prospecting, making a customer, marketing that customer, and keeping the friendship going for their benefits and better your profits.

As Howard Schultz, the legendary founder of Starbucks, stated, ***"We are not in the coffee business serving people; we are in the people business serving coffee."***

So, despite the many disruptions happening, we in sales will always remain in the people business, and we should strive to forge long-lasting relationship as a buyer and seller for many long years of continuity.

In fact, the people business holds more relevance, especially in markets like the Middle East and Africa, where emphasis is given more on the person we deal with before the offering of the services and then the company he or she represents.

So, if the hurdle of mutual trust is surpassed by the salesperson, automatically the salesperson is much sought after to resolve problems and offer solutions.

In my almost 27 years of experience in the field of sales and serving diverse markets, I can confidently state that in the Middle East and Africa, sales is a natural process and **developing relationship is the precursor to make it happen**.

The emphasis always should remain on developing relationship. So, while visiting a new prospect, we should start with small talk as ice breakers before leading to the main topic to make the buyer more comfortable and then lead to the more complex part of the discussion.

In many accounts during my life as a sales representative, I could overcome herculean challenges with an emphasis on the relationship selling concept most of the time and could derive mileage with the long-standing relationship in an account, whether with the old employee or starting with a new employee.

And last but not least, keep the habit of listening actively as this may unravel the many facets of the buyer, account, and the overall needs.

In the next chapter, I would align how trust and relationship can be fostered using neuroscience in selling.

So, to conclude this part, I would recommend, while starting in a new account/company and a new relationship with the buyer, my advice would be to strictly avoid venturing into topics like politics, religion, stereotyping, or on ethnicity as these may be quite uncomfortable for your host and you may end up in aborting a new relationship rather than cultivating it for long.

To conclude, invest in developing relationships and business will follow.

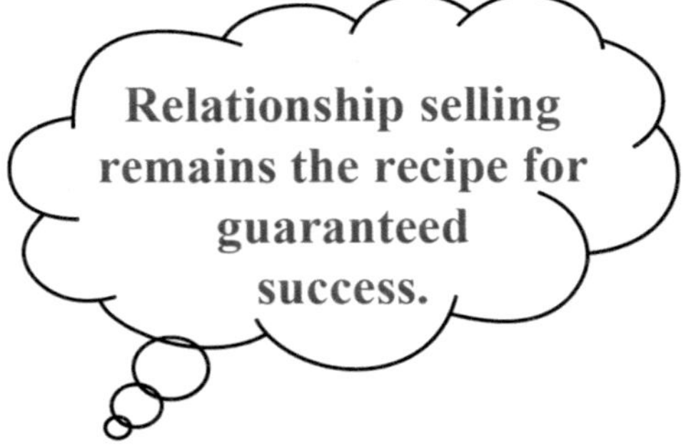

Neuroscience in Selling

A lot of theories are propounded about whether selling is an art or science. What do you think?

Well, I would state that it's a mix of both. Whilst selling remains an art, it also has a scientific premise, and this part of the chapter would cover more on the scientific paradigm.

To understand the concept, lets us dwell on the most complex part of human anatomy, and that's the brain. Let us understand it in detail, as illustrated in the diagram below.

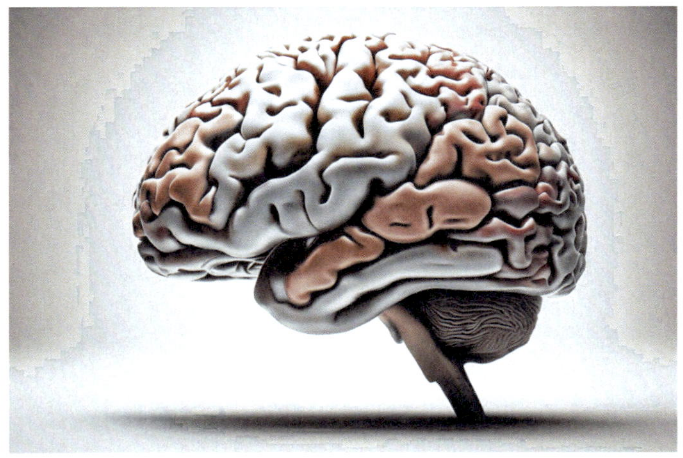

A human brain comprises of three parts.

1. Neocortex: "Thinking Brain" which is more rational, logical, and analytically driven by the processing of facts and data.
2. Limbic: "Feeling brain" is more emotional and values feelings, visualization, and kinaesthetic part.
3. Stem or root: "Instinctive brain" is a part of the brain involving decisions related to survival, safety, hunger, and thirst.

During human interaction, encounters, and related decisions, it's the limbic brain which remains at the forefront of the decision-making process.

In the neurolinguistics selling concept, it tries to evoke an emotional connect followed by covering the data and logical part of the conversation.

So, you would question, how do we evoke the emotional connect with a stranger or a prospect? This is answered in the hormonal chemistry.

Let us understand the hormonal systems in humans and a few of the common hormones I would like to highlight below.

1. Serotonin – Hormone of well-being.
2. Dopamine – Hormone of happiness.
3. Epinephrine – Hormone of energy.
4. Oxytocin – Hormone of trust.
5. Cortisol – Hormone of stress.

If you scrutinize these hormonal systems play in our daily lives, I will state that in sales interactions it's the cortisol, oxytocin, and dopamine remain at the forefront.

The sales representative should strive to evoke the oxytocin secretion, that's the trust in the counterpart, which might be instantaneous through an action like securing the product supply, offering a prompt offer, rebate, or customer service or it may also take some periodic interaction to cultivate a complete trust.

It is also imperative to reduce cortisol, the stress hormone, which may help to develop a trustful and long-lasting business relationship.

After many years, I realize the role neuroscience has played in my routine encounters with clients.

Questions or imploring the clients to place an order, so that I do not miss my monthly sales targets or KPIs were stimulating the limbic brain of my counterpart and evoking emotions.

The interaction and the episode in Oman on the wrong tile supply and its corrective action are another example of the Limbic brain in action during the final decision of retaining the wrong tiles supplied.

Remember, try to reduce the stress hormone cortisol, and improve the Oxytocin level in any business relationship, as this will keep the secretion of Dopamine, or happiness, lasting forever in the relationship.

Finally, always remember the ABC of selling, that's Always be Closing!

I want to dedicate this book to the sales professionals who endure rough times and tough situations to remain focused on the objective to generate sales and revenue for the company by giving one's time, mind, sweat, heart, and some unlucky ones of their blood by any eventuality during the call of duty.

Hence, I narrate a short poem penned by me below, dedicated to the anonymous sales representative on the field, weathering all obstacles to remain productive.

One day it's sunshine the other day it's rain.
In the challenging times, it's more of a pain than a gain.
Despite all odds, I shall prevail, as life has to flow and smiles on the faces need to glow.

Before I bring this to a conclusion, I would like to recommend two of my favorite movies as a must-watch for every salesperson, as they remain an a visual manual for sales and marketing professionals.

1. The *Pursuit of Happyness*: The biopic of Christopher Gardner enacted by Will Smith of a homeless salesperson selling bone density meters life remains a day-to-day struggle for him to meet ends to pay his bills.

He finally succeeds by overcoming monumental odds with a broken marriage and becoming a pauper financially in life. It is very touching to view it on the celluloid.

This stage in life is followed by the journey of securing an internship in a brokerage firm and then never looking back in life.

The cold calling techniques enacted by Will Smith in the movie are quintessential traits to be followed if practical by salesperson to remain effective.

2. The Founder: The story of McDonald's and its founder, Ray Kroc, is phenomenal, with Michael Keaton playing the role of Ray Kroc nailing it perfectly.

The word persistence and its relevance in competitive business are quite motivational which appear in the movie trailer and always lingers in my mind.

I wish to thank you from the bottom of my heart for your precious time dedicated to reading the book.

All images and illustrations in this document are sourced from Pixabay.

Sachin Arte e-mail:
sachin_arte@yahoo.co.in

LinkedIn:
https://www.linkedin.com/in/sachin-arte-1329777